Macmillan/McGraw-Hill Science

An Australian thorny
devil lizard

A king snake

Living Things Grow & Change

Authors

Mary Atwater
The University of Georgia

Prentice Baptiste
University of Houston

Lucy Daniel
Rutherford County Schools

Jay Hackett
University of Northern Colorado

Richard Moyer
University of Michigan, Dearborn

Carol Takemoto
Los Angeles Unified School District

Nancy Wilson
Sacremento Unified School District

The endangered
white rhino in Africa

Macmillan/McGraw-Hill School Publishing Company
New York   Chicago   Columbus

MACMILLAN / McGRAW-HILL

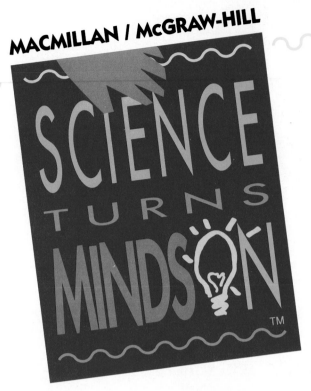

SCIENCE TURNS MINDS ON™

CONSULTANTS

Assessment:

Janice M. Camplin
Curriculum Coordinator, Elementary Science
Mentor, Western New York
Lake Shore Central Schools
Angola, NY

Mary Hamm
Associate Professor
Department of Elementary Education
San Francisco State University
San Francisco, CA

Cognitive Development:

Dr. Elisabeth Charron
Assistant Professor of Science Education
Montana State University
Bozeman, MT

Sue Teele
Director of Education Extension
University of California, Riverside
Riverside, CA

Cooperative Learning:

Harold Pratt
Executive Director of Curriculum
Jefferson County Public Schools
Golden, CO

Earth Science:

Thomas A. Davies
Research Scientist
The University of Texas
Austin, TX

David G. Futch
Associate Professor of Biology
San Diego State University
San Diego, CA

Dr. Shadia Rifai Habbal
Harvard-Smithsonian Center for Astrophysics
Cambridge, MA

Tom Murphree, Ph.D.
Global Systems Studies
Monterey, CA

Suzanne O'Connell
Assistant Professor
Wesleyan University
Middletown, CT

Environmental Education:

Cheryl Charles, Ph.D.
Executive Director
Project Wild
Boulder, CO

Gifted:

Sandra N. Kaplan
Associate Director, National/State Leadership
Training Institute on the Gifted/Talented
Ventura County Superintendent of Schools Office
Northridge, CA

Global Education:

M. Eugene Gilliom
Professor of Social Studies and Global Education
The Ohio State University
Columbus, OH

Merry M. Merryfield
Assistant Professor of Social Studies and Global Education
The Ohio State University
Columbus, OH

Intermediate Specialist

Sharon L. Strating
Missouri State Teacher of the Year
Northwest Missouri State University
Marysville, MO

Life Science:

Carl D. Barrentine
Associate Professor of Biology
California State University
Bakersfield, CA

V.L. Holland
Professor and Chair, Biological Sciences Department
California Polytechnic State University
San Luis Obispo, CA

Donald C. Lisowy
Education Specialist
New York, NY

Dan B. Walker
Associate Dean for Science Education and Professor of Biology
San Jose State University
San Jose, CA

Literature:

Dr. Donna E. Norton
Texas A&M University
College Station, TX

Tina Thoburn, Ed.D.
President
Thoburn Educational Enterprises, Inc.
Ligonier, PA

Macmillan/McGraw-Hill School Division
10 Union Square East
New York, New York 10003

Printed in the United States of America

ISBN 0-02-274260-3 / 3

3 4 5 6 7 8 9 VHJ 99 98 97 96 95 94 93

Wildflowers

Mathematics:

Martin L. Johnson
Professor, Mathematics Education
University of Maryland at College Park
College Park, MD

Physical Science:

Max Diem, Ph.D.
Professor of Chemistry
City University of New York, Hunter College
New York, NY

Gretchen M. Gillis
Geologist
Maxus Exploration Company
Dallas, TX

Wendell H. Potter
Associate Professor of Physics
Department of Physics
University of California, Davis
Davis, CA

Claudia K. Viehland
Educational Consultant, Chemist
Sigma Chemical Company
St. Louis, MO

Reading:

Jean Wallace Gillet
Reading Teacher
Charlottesville Public Schools
Charlottesville, VA

Charles Temple, Ph. D.
Associate Professor of Education
Hobart and William Smith Colleges
Geneva, NY

Safety:

Janice Sutkus
Program Manager: Education

National Safety Council
Chicago, IL

Science Technology and Society (STS):

William C. Kyle, Jr.
Director, School Mathematics and Science Center
Purdue University
West Lafayette, IN

Social Studies:

Mary A. McFarland
Instructional Coordinator of Social Studies, K-12, and Director of Staff Development
Parkway School District
St. Louis, MO

Students Acquiring English:

Mrs. Bronwyn G. Frederick, M.A.
Bilingual Teacher
Pomona Unified School District
Pomona, CA

Misconceptions:

Dr. Charles W. Anderson
Michigan State University
East Lansing, MI

Dr. Edward L. Smith
Michigan State University
East Lansing, MI

Multicultural:

Bernard L. Charles
Senior Vice President
Quality Education for Minorities Network
Washington, DC

Cheryl Willis Hudson
Graphic Designer and Publishing Consultant
Part Owner and Publisher, Just Us Books, Inc.
Orange, NJ

Paul B. Janeczko
Poet
Hebron, MA

James R. Murphy
Math Teacher
La Guardia High School
New York, NY

Ramon L. Santiago
Professor of Education and Director of ESL
Lehman College, City University of New York
Bronx, NY

Clifford E. Trafzer
Professor and Chair, Ethnic Studies
University of California, Riverside
Riverside, CA

STUDENT ACTIVITY TESTERS

Jennifer Kildow
Brooke Straub
Cassie Zistl
Betsy McKeown
Seth McLaughlin
Max Berry
Wayne Henderson

FIELD TEST TEACHERS

Sharon Ervin
San Pablo Elementary School
Jacksonville, FL

Michelle Gallaway
Indianapolis Public School #44
Indianapolis, IN

Kathryn Gallman
#7 School
Rochester, NY

Karla McBride
#44 School
Rochester, NY

Diane Pease
Leopold Elementary
Madison, WI

Kathy Perez
Martin Luther King Elementary
Jacksonville, FL

Ralph Stamler
Thoreau School
Madison, WI

Joanne Stern
Hilltop Elementary School
Glen Burnie, MD

Janet Young
Indianapolis Public School #90
Indianapolis, IN

CONTRIBUTING WRITER

Teresa Vitale

Living Things Grow and Change

Activities!

Features

 Links

Departments

Living Things Grow and Change

The world you live in is full of many, many things. There are rocks, trees, horses, and much more. Everything in the world is either living or nonliving. But what does it mean to be living?

Minds On! What would Earth be like if there weren't any living things on it? It's hard to imagine, but give it a try. Close your eyes and imagine your neighborhood. Now pretend that you have an eraser. Erase everything that you think is living from that picture in your mind. What's left? ●

How did you know which things to erase? A lot of things were easy to decide, weren't they? Other things are more difficult. You can see a cat moving around, making noises and eating. You know it is living. But is a car living also? It moves around, makes noises, and needs gasoline doesn't it? Sometimes you have to look more closely to tell if a thing is living.

When you try to decide if something is living, you decide the same way a scientist does. Scientists try to understand how things work. There are different ways scientists solve problems. These ways are **scientific methods**. In the next activity, you can use one of these scientific methods to help you decide if something is living or nonliving.

TRY THIS

Activity!

Is the Mealworm the Real "Worm"?

What You Need
mealworm, rubber worm, *Activity Log*, page 1

Place both the mealworm and the rubber worm on a piece of paper. The problem you will try to solve is, "Which of the two 'worms' is living?" To help you solve this problem, follow the steps on the following pages.

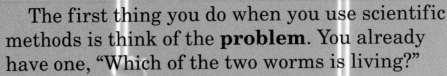

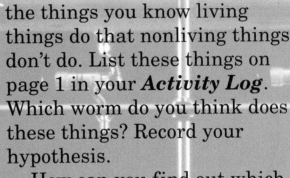

The first thing you do when you use scientific methods is think of the **problem**. You already have one, "Which of the two worms is living?"

The next step is to make a hypothesis (hī poth´ ə sis) to answer the problem. A **hypothesis** is a guess you make, using everything you already know about the problem. To help you make your hypothesis, think about the things you know living things do that nonliving things don't do. List these things on page 1 in your *Activity Log*. Which worm do you think does these things? Record your hypothesis.

How can you find out which worm really does the things you've listed? Scientists figure out ways to **experiment** (ek sper´ ə mənt) with, or test their hypothesis. Your experiments might be as simple as just watching both worms to see if either does or does not do any of the things you've listed.

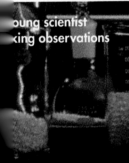

oung scientist
king observations

When you are experimenting, it is important to look for only one thing at a time. If you want to test to see which worm moves, for example, don't test to see if it eats at the same time. You want to **control** what you're looking for. As you are testing your hypothesis, do the same things to both worms.

While you are doing the experiments to test your hypothesis, it is very important to **record** what you see. You should draw pictures, record measurements, and list anything else that you see during your experiments so you don't forget them.

After you have finished all of your experiments, you should look at everything you wrote down. Check the things on your list to see which worm did those things. This is when you draw **conclusions** (kən klü´ zhənz) based on your observations. You decide if your hypothesis was right or wrong by looking at your observations. Was your guess right or wrong? What observations could show your guess was right or wrong?

Young scientists drawing conclusions

Scientists will often guess wrong. But by doing the experiments, they will learn something new about the problem they are working on.

People have studied living things using methods like this for a long time. By studying living and nonliving things, we have a better idea of what it means to be living. There are certain characteristics that all living things have. In this unit you will explore these characteristics and find out what you share with all other living things.

Science in Literature

What do living things do? What do they need? What are they made of? These are questions people have been trying to answer for centuries. You can answer some of these questions by reading a book. Books can teach you about plants and animals from faraway places. You can see pictures of organisms many people never see.

The Mountain That Loved a Bird
by Alice McLerran.

Saxonville, MA: Picture Book Studio, 1985.

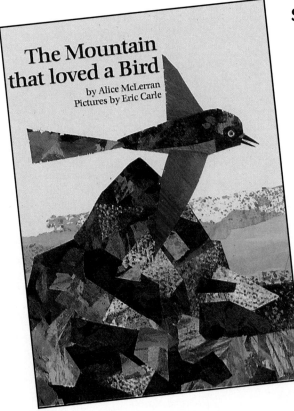

This is the tale of a friendship between a mountain and a bird named Joy. "Couldn't you just stay here?" asked the mountain. As much as Joy liked the mountain, she had to say no. In this wonderful story, read and learn why Joy couldn't stay with her friend.

The Big Tree
by Bruce Hiscock.

New York: Atheneum, 1991.

If you've ever enjoyed the shade, or climbed the branches of an old tree, you'll like this book. Bruce Hiscock takes you into the past when a maple seed flutters to the forest floor. You'll see the young seedling grow and develop into a huge tree. Read this story and learn what the tree lives through.

Other Good Books To Read

Under Your Feet by Joanne Ryder.
New York: Four Winds Press, 1990.

After reading this book, you'll realize there's more than just grass and dirt beneath your feet!

A Flower Grows by Ken Robbins.
New York: Dial Books, 1990.

Robbins leads you step by step through the growth of a flower. Read and watch amazing beauty develop from an ugly bulb!

Animal Life by Karen O'Callaghan and Kate Londesborough.
Newmarket, England: Brimax Books, 1988.

Where are animals born? Where do they sleep in winter? How do they avoid enemies? The beautiful photographs and fascinating information will help answer these questions.

Your backyard is a world full of activity. Living things are busy doing what they need to do to live. Insects buzz around looking for food. Dandelions grow, making fuzzy seeds that float in the wind. Birds fly to safety when you get near them.

What Do Living Things Do?

An ant

Have you ever watched an ant colony? You know that even though they're small, ants are very busy animals. They hurry around, carrying, dragging, and lifting things much larger than they are. When you see them, you know right away they are living things.

The grass around the ants is living, too. But even if you watch it for a long time, it never seems to do anything. Does the grass have anything in common with the ants? Do they do any of the same things?

Minds On! Look at the living things in the photographs on this page. In your *Activity Log* on page 2, list the name of each living thing you see. Now write down three things that each does. Do any of them do the same things? ●

Activity!

What Do Mealworms Do?

You may have already seen the mealworms doing different things. But in what ways do they change? You will explore the mealworm for the next two weeks while trying to answer the question, "What do mealworms do at different times in their lives?"

What You Need

5 mealworms   wide-mouthed jar

Activity Log pages 3-4

potato

bran

hand lens

What To Do

1 Pour 5 cm of bran into the jar. Add a potato piece. Carefully place 5 mealworms in the jar. Store the jar in a warm place when you're not observing the mealworms. Add a new piece of potato every week.

2 In your *Activity Log,* make a hypothesis to explain the answer to the question, "What do mealworms do at different times in their lives?"

3 Decide how you will test your hypothesis. When experimenting with the mealworms, never do anything that might injure them.

4 Now, do the experiments, making sure you record your observations and draw pictures of the mealworms in your *Activity Log.*

5 After two weeks, use your observations to decide if your hypothesis was right or wrong.

6 Compare your results with the results of the other groups. Ask what their hypotheses were and find out what they did to test them. If a group had the same hypothesis, did they get the same results you did?

What Happened?

1. How did your mealworms change during the two weeks?
2. What did your mealworms do differently at different times of their lives?

What Now?

1. What other living things change in some way over time?
2. How could you test to see if another living thing does the same things as the mealworm at different times in its life?

Looking Ahead

Later in this unit, you will be exploring the mealworms further. Add a new piece of potato to the jar every week. You may need to add bran as well.

EXPLORE

Living Things Grow and Develop

In the Explore Activity you probably observed mealworms doing different things during the two weeks. One may have changed the way it moved, or the way it looked. The mealworms changed because they grew and developed.

Living things are **organisms** (ôr´ gə niz´ əmz). When an organism **grows**, it gets larger. Some things grow quickly, in just a day or two. But other things may take years to grow. A young tree keeps growing for many years and gets very large. Besides getting taller, many trees grow leaves that fall off every year.

But organisms do more than get larger. They change, too. The way a living thing changes during its life is called **development** (di vel´ əp mənt). When things develop, they may look different or do different things.

This crawling caterpillar...

develops into a beautiful monarch butterfly.

You've probably heard the tale of the ugly duckling. Everyone made fun of the duckling because it was uglier than the others. As it grew, it developed into a graceful swan.

The featherless wings of this young bird...

develop into strong wings that carry the crane through the sky.

Even the mealworms you investigated will someday develop into beetles.

TRY THIS Activity!

Changing Seeds

What You Need

paper towel, clear plastic jar, 6 lima bean seeds, water, *Activity Log* page 5.

Just like other living things, plants develop too. Fold a piece of paper towel in half. Roll it and slip it inside the cup. Slide six seeds between the paper towel and the cup so you can see them. Keeping the paper towel moist, check the seeds every day for a week. Draw a picture of the seeds every day you observe them. Compare the pictures you drew. How did the seeds change?

Literature Link
The Big Tree

Have you ever sat in the shade of a big, old tree on a hot day? Maybe you've wondered how old the tree is and who else may have played under it, years ago. In the book, *The Big Tree*, you can read about the history of one such old tree.

Then find a tree of your own. Imagine you are the tree. Write a story about what you may have seen as you grew. Start when the tree was a seedling and end as it looks now.

Living Things Reproduce

In addition, living things **reproduce** (rē´ prə düs´), or make new living things that are just like them. Reproduction is very important because all living things die sooner or later. By reproducing, organisms make new organisms to take their places when they die. If this didn't happen, it wouldn't be long before there were no more living things on Earth!

Watermelon plants, for example, make seeds that become new watermelon plants.

This puffball reproduces by releasing thousands of tiny particles called spores (spôrz).

Living Things Respond

TRY THIS Activity!

Mealworm Reactions!

What You Need

mealworms, piece of paper, *Activity Log* page 6

Let's investigate the mealworms a little further. With your partner, get a couple of your mealworms out and place them on a piece of paper on your desk. Let them start to crawl.

Gently touch one on the head with your finger. What did the mealworm do? Try it again. Did it do the same thing? Try other ways to make the mealworm do the same thing. Be careful not to injure the mealworm. Record your observations in your *Activity Log.*

Like the mealworm, all living things respond. A **response** (ri spons´) is something a living thing does when its environment changes.

When a squirrel sees a dog, it responds by running to safety in a tree.

A dog responds to seeing a squirrel by barking.

This tree responds to the seasons.

Like other living things, plants respond to a change in their environments, too. In autumn the weather turns cooler and there are fewer hours of daylight. This causes the leaves on the trees to begin to change color and then fall off. The trees are responding to their environment. In spring the weather gets warmer and there are more hours of daylight. Trees respond by growing leaves again.

You Are a Living Thing

The squirrel, the dog, and the tree are all different. However, they do some of the same things. You may not realize it, but you have some things in common with all of them!

Just as a puppy develops into an adult dog, you also are developing. You are growing and developing, even though it may not seem like it to you.

TRY THIS Activity!

How Have You Changed?

What You Need
pictures of yourself at different ages, *Activity Log* page 7

Have you changed during your life? Try to find as many old pictures of yourself as you can. Arrange them in order by how old you were when the pictures were taken. How have you changed? Ask your parents or another adult for pictures of them when they were your age. How have they changed since they were the same age as you?

Everyone in this family has changed a lot in their lives. What would these people look like if they didn't grow and develop?

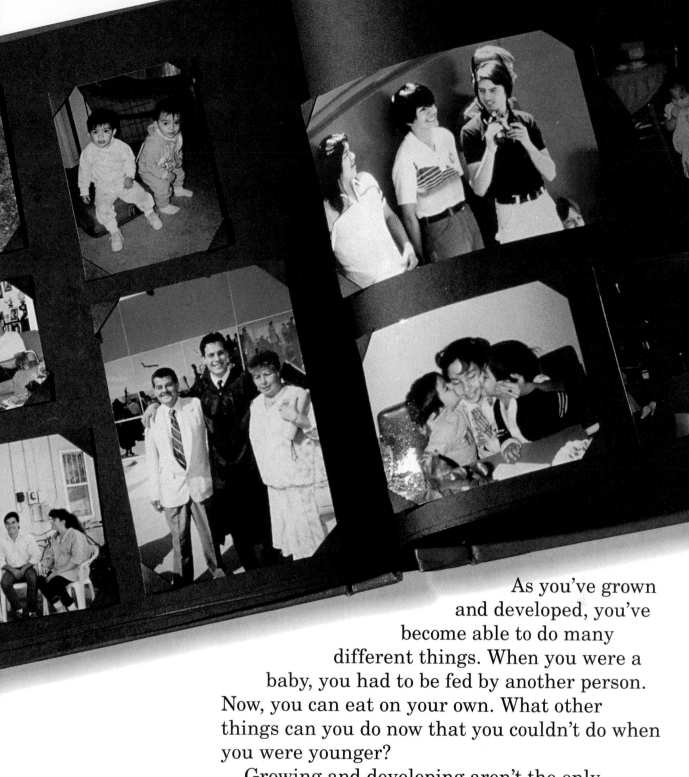

As you've grown and developed, you've become able to do many different things. When you were a baby, you had to be fed by another person. Now, you can eat on your own. What other things can you do now that you couldn't do when you were younger?

Growing and developing aren't the only things you do that make you the same as other living things. Like the mealworms you studied, you also respond to things in your environment.

You sweat, shiver, sneeze, squint, and have many other responses.

Standing in line to ride an amusement park ride can make your body respond in several ways. As you get closer to the ride, your heart begins to beat faster and your muscles get tense. Once you get on the ride, you might begin to sweat and your eyes open wider. These are all normal responses to scary things.

Are you allergic to anything? **Allergic** (ə lûr´ jik) means that your body has a severe response to something that is harmless to others. Many people are allergic to something. Poison ivy, pollen, some food, and some animals cause people to have an allergic response. You may get a rash, or start sneezing, or get a runny nose.

Allergist

If you have an allergy, you might go to an allergist. An **allergist** (al´ ər jist) is a doctor who finds people's allergies. Often people get a rash, or start to sneeze a lot and can't figure out why. An allergist will use scientific methods to find out what is causing it. They then will recommend how to treat the allergies. Hopefully, your body will respond to the treatment.

To be an allergist you have to get a college degree and then go to medical school.

Sum It Up

Every organism, no matter how large or small, does things that all organisms do. They grow and develop, respond to their surroundings, and reproduce. Organisms do these things at different times in their lives. As they develop, living things change the way they respond, and grow. Most organisms reproduce only at certain times in their lives.

Critical Thinking

1. Is a rock a living thing? Why or why not?
2. Would a penguin in Antarctica respond to cold temperatures in the same way as a flamingo would? How do you think the penguin and the flamingo would respond to hot temperatures?
3. On a cold day you might see icicles that have grown from the roof of a building. Does this mean icicles are living? Why or why not?

All organisms, including you, need several things to live. What kind of things do you need? How do you know when you need them?

A scuba diver observing a grouper

What Living Things Need

It's a hot day and you've been playing for hours. Your mouth and throat feel dry and scratchy. Soon, all you can think about is a glass of cold water. You're thirsty and your body needs water.

If you swim on a hot day, your body sends different signals. Although there is plenty of water, your body needs something else. It needs air.

Minds On! Think about the last time you swam underwater. Why couldn't you stay underwater for very long? What did it feel like when you had to come up for air? ●

Water and air are only two of the things all organisms need to live. In this next activity, you will explore some other needs of living things.

EXPLORE Activity!

Water Zoo!

What do living things need to survive? To find out, you will be creating a small water "zoo." You will have to make sure the zoo has everything it needs.

What You Need

Activity Log pages 8-9

fish food

water

gravel

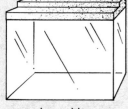

aquarium with cover

4 elodea plants

2 3-inch pots

2 guppies

2 snails

What To Do

1 As a class, have your teacher help you set up an aquarium. Place the pots on their sides with a little gravel inside them to hold them in place.

2 Anchor the elodea plants in the gravel. Add water, then carefully place the snails and the guppies in the tank.

3 Observe the guppies as you put them in the tank. What did they do? Keep watching them for 15 minutes and record your observations in your *Activity Log.*

4 Twice a week, feed the guppies. Feed one very small flake of fish food for each guppy. What did the guppies do when they discovered the food?

5 With a small group, decide what the plants, the snails, and the guppies need to survive. Are they getting what they need? How? If not, how can you give them what they need?

6 Observe the living things in your aquarium every day for at least a week. Record what they do.

What Happened?

1. What did the snails eat?
2. Where did the snails and the guppies get the air they needed to live?

What Now?

1. Predict what would happen to the plants if you covered the aquarium so it didn't get any light.
2. Predict what would happen if you put more guppies in the tank, but only fed them two flakes of food.

Living Things Need Energy

The living things in your water zoo needed several things to live. They needed oxygen, food, shelter, and water. The plants in your zoo had slightly different needs. They needed sunlight in order for them to get energy.

You've seen that living organisms grow, develop, and respond during their lives. But where do they get the energy they need to do it all? Just as a car needs fuel, living things need energy to do what they need to do.

Minds On! How much "fuel" do you need? On page 10 in your *Activity Log*, keep track of everything you eat for a whole day. Record snacks and what you drink, too. Why do you think we need to eat so much food? ●

2 They need a lot of energy and they get it by eating the nectar from the blossoms. Organisms that need to get their food from other living things are **consumers** (kən sü´ mərz).

1 If you've ever seen a hummingbird, chances are you saw it eating. As they dart from flower to flower, their wings move so fast, all you see is a blur!

A hummingbird feeding

Literature Link
The Mountain that Loved a Bird

In Alice McLerran's book, *The Mountain that Loved a Bird*, a bird named Joy has to make sure she gets what she needs to live. Read this book and learn what Joy needs to live.

With a partner, plan a performance in which one of you plays Joy and the other plays the mountain. Draw pictures of the things that the mountain had at the end of the story that allowed Joy to stay.

TRY THIS

Activity!
The Need for Sunlight

What You Need
2 medium-sized plants, *Activity Log* page 11

To see how a plant needs sunlight, put one plant in a place where it will get plenty of sunlight. Place the other plant where it will get no light. Every day, check both plants and compare them. Record your observations in your ***Activity Log.*** How does the plant kept in the dark look compared to the other plant?

If the hummingbird gets energy from the flowers, where do these flowers get the energy they need? They get it from food they make! Living things that can make their own food are **producers** (prə dü´ sərz). Most producers use energy from sunlight to help them make food.

Activity!

Leaf Life

What You Need

2 leaves from the same houseplant, water, 2 cups, *Activity Log* page 12.

Do plants need water? To find out, put each leaf in a cup. Add water to one cup so the stem is in the water. Predict what will happen to each leaf. Observe both leaves for three days and record your observations. How did they change? Why did the two leaves look different?

Living Things Need Water

Even if an organism gets all of the energy it needs, it won't be able to live without water. While living things are made mostly of water, many live in it, too.

Have you ever picked some fresh flowers and put them in a vase with water? Why do you need to do this? In the activity on the left you will see what happens when a leaf doesn't get water.

A tortoise getting water from a cactus.

30

The Need for Oxygen and Space

Like many living things, you can live for a few days without food or water. Without oxygen (ok´ sə jən) that's in air, you would die in just a few minutes. **Oxygen** is a gas that is in air and water. Organisms that live in water get oxygen from the water.

When they make food, plants produce more oxygen than they need. Other living things use this extra oxygen.

Both plants and animals need oxygen to get the energy they need from food.

Animals and other living things get oxygen from the air or water around them.

An organism lives in a place where it can find food and water. In the desert, there is not much water. A cactus that lives there needs a lot of space so it gets enough water to live.

Plants in a desert

Conserving the Needs of Living Things

Earth

Energy, water, air, space—the needs of living things are all important. Not getting any one of them can mean death for any organism.

Fortunately, Earth has all of these things. The sun provides the energy for plants to make food. The surface of Earth is covered with plenty of water. There is also a lot of air surrounding this large, roomy planet. All living things depend on what Earth has.

A pair of endangered whales

An endangered indri in Madagascar

It may seem like there is more than enough water and air. But there is a limited amount of all of these things. It is also possible to make them unusable. This is why we must conserve them. **Conserving** (kən sûrv´ ing) means to protect Earth's materials from being lost or ruined. For living things to survive, what they get from Earth must be conserved.

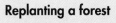
Replanting a forest

There are many ways that people conserve Earth's resources. Some try to figure out how to reduce water pollution. Others conserve water by figuring out how to use less of it.

Air is conserved in different ways, too. Reducing the pollution from factories has been a concern for a long time. Now people are understanding that Earth's forests are important in cleaning the air.

Communities all over the world are getting together and cleaning up beaches, roadways, and parks. People are learning ways to dispose properly of chemicals such as old paint, motor oil, and cleansers.

Volunteers cleaning up a beach.

There are many things you can do to help conserve Earth's resources. You can turn off the faucet when you brush your teeth to save water. Or you can recycle and find other uses for paper, cans, and glass.

These are only a few ways you can conserve. If you would like to do more, there are many local and national organizations that can help you get more involved.

The international organization, the United Nations, has made conservation one of its concerns. Because we all depend on this planet, everyone needs to help protect it.

Sum It Up

Like a car that's out of fuel, organisms can do nothing without energy. Organisms must have the energy they get from food to grow, develop, respond, and reproduce. They need oxygen to help them get the energy from food. They also need water, and space.

Critical Thinking

1. What would happen to consumers if plants could not make their own food? Why do you think that?

2. Do living things need each other? How?

3. What do you think living things need most—air, water, food, or sunlight? Explain your answer.

35

Living things have different parts. Arms, legs, leaves, and roots are some parts you may know about. All organisms have parts that look different and do different things.

Birds from around the world at the American Natural History Museum

36

What Are Living Things Made Of?

Skeletons of birds

A natural history museum is a great place to go if you want to see what many different organisms look like. Walking through the exhibits, you can see organisms made with many kinds of parts. You'll see claws, beaks, leaves, fangs, and heads that are hard to imagine!

Minds On! Look at this display of different birds. What makes them different? Why don't they all have the same parts? ●

In the next activity, you'll examine some parts of an organism to see what they do.

Activity!

Take a Close Look

You have observed what living things do. But have you looked at what they're made of? In this activity, you will explore the parts of different living things.

What You Need

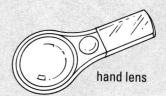

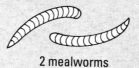

hand lens

Activity Log pages 13-14

white paper

mushroom

plant with roots

2 mealworms

What To Do

1 Cover your work area with a piece of white paper.

2 Place a mealworm, a mushroom, and a plant with roots next to each other on the paper.

3 Look at the organisms and write or draw in your *Activity Log* the parts you can see.

4 Using the hand lens, look more closely at the three living things. Draw or describe any new parts you find.

5 Watch the mealworm and try to find out what its parts do. Record your results in your *Activity Log.*

What Happened?

1. Which organism had the most parts?
2. What was the smallest part you saw? What was the biggest?

What Now?

1. Predict what parts are inside the organisms.
2. What parts do you think each organism could live without?

EXPLORE

39

An elephant's trunk

Big Parts

A Water strider

Every organism, from the tiniest tick to the tallest tree, is made of parts. The three living things you looked at were all made of parts. The mealworm had legs, the plant had leaves, and the mushroom had a stem.

The parts of living things come in many shapes and sizes. The trunk of an elephant is big. The mouth of a fly is small. The tentacles of an octopus are long and skinny. Leaves can be many shapes.

A king snake

Math  Link

Shape Up!

There are many shapes in the parts of living things. You can see triangles, squares, and circles in them. How many shapes can you find in the parts in the picture? What parts have the same kind of shape? In your *Activity Log* on page 15, draw the shapes of the parts you find.

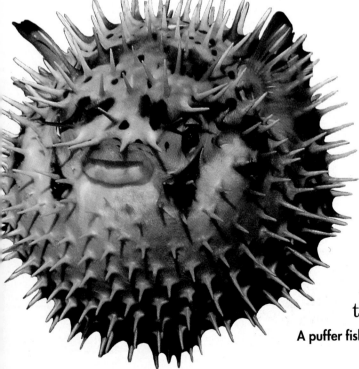

A puffer fish

If living things are made of parts, what are the parts made of? Look at your arm. It is one of your parts, but what is it made of?

The first thing you see is the skin. But under the skin are bones and muscles. The bones, muscles, and skin are all parts. Your parts are made of smaller parts.

Minds On! An apple is a part of an apple tree. What is an apple made of? Bite into one and see what parts you can find. ●

TRY THIS

Activity!

What's in There?

What You Need
mirror, *Activity Log* page 16

How well do you know your mouth? What parts does it have? Look in a mirror and draw or describe the parts you find. How many did you see? Have you always had all of these parts? How do you know?

Tiny Parts

Let's look more closely at the parts that go together to make living things. Look at the back of your hand. Look very closely. No matter how closely you look, you still won't be able to see all the parts of your hand with just your eyes. The smallest parts you can see are made of many more parts that are even smaller. These smallest parts are cells. **Cells** are the basic building blocks of all organisms. The roots of a plant are made of cells. The legs of the mealworm are made of cells. Your tongue is made of cells.

Making a structure out of wooden blocks

Cells make up parts like bricks make up a wall. Using the same bricks, you can build walls of different shapes and sizes. Cells are much smaller than bricks, though. To get an idea of how small they are, try the next activity.

Activity!

Get To Know the Back of Your Hand!

What You Need

fine-point pen, bag of dry navy beans, hand lens, *Activity Log* page 17

With a pen, make the smallest dot you can on the back of your hand. Using a hand lens, look closely at the skin around the dot and draw what you see. Get together with four classmates. Then each of you count out 10 groups of 10 beans (500 beans total). Carefully place all of your beans together in a solid circle. Now imagine the circle is the dot you drew on your hand. Each bean represents a cell. This is about how many cells you would find in the dot you drew on the back of your hand.

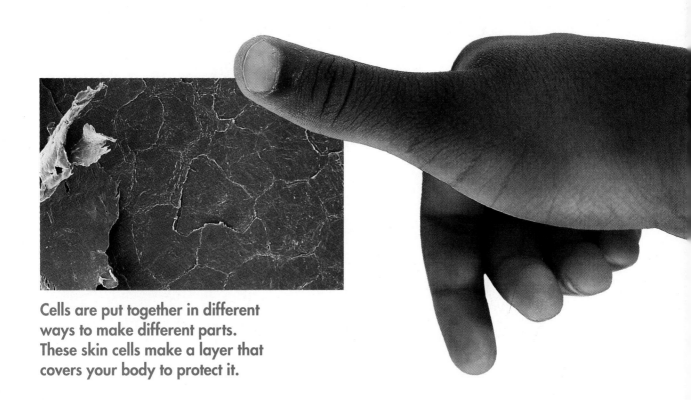

Cells are put together in different ways to make different parts. These skin cells make a layer that covers your body to protect it.

What Do Parts Do?

Living things have all of these parts for a reason. The parts help them to do the things they need to do. Plants, like other living things, need water to live. They also need sunlight. Each part of the plant does something different for it.

The leaves convert energy from sunlight to make food.

The stem connects the roots and leaves.

An onion plant

The roots get water and minerals from the soil.

Minds On! Look at the different parts you found in your mouth. What do you think they do? How do they help you live? ●

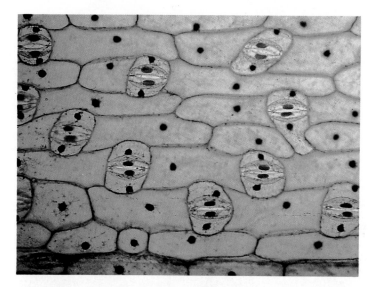

There are different types of cells in a leaf. These are cells that let carbon dioxide inside the plant.

The cells that make up a part do things, too. Together, they do the job the part needs to do for the organism.

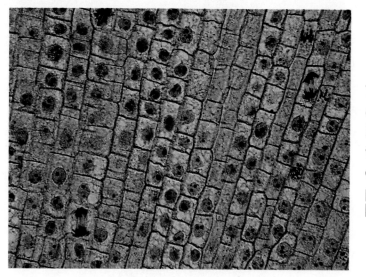

The cells in the roots of a plant are different from those in the leaves. Some cells transport the water up to the rest of the plant. Other root cells get water and minerals for the plant. These root cells increase the length of the root.

There are some organisms that are made of only one cell. That means the one cell has to do everything the organism needs to do to live.

An amoeba (ə mē′ bə)

Parts Working Together

Like the parts on a wind-up toy airplane, the parts of a living thing must work together. If the propeller is broken, the plane won't fly. In a plant, if the roots are broken and can't get water, the plant will die.

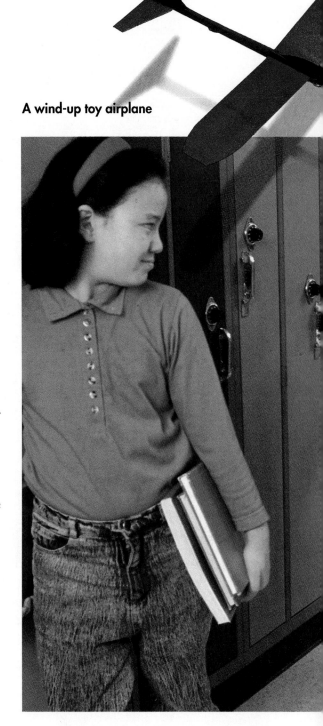

A wind-up toy airplane

Health ⊙ Link
Every Little Part Counts!

You also depend on all of your parts. If one of your parts isn't working well, the rest of you will not work well, either. Even a small part can make a big difference in how you feel. A sore throat, an earache, or even a cut on your toe can change how you live.

With a partner, name a part of the body. Imagine that part is sick or injured. Together, decide how that part might make other parts of your body not work well, either. Describe or act out what would be different in your daily life.

If you've ever broken a leg, you know how your life changes. Carrying things becomes difficult while your arms are busy holding crutches. What else becomes difficult when you need crutches?

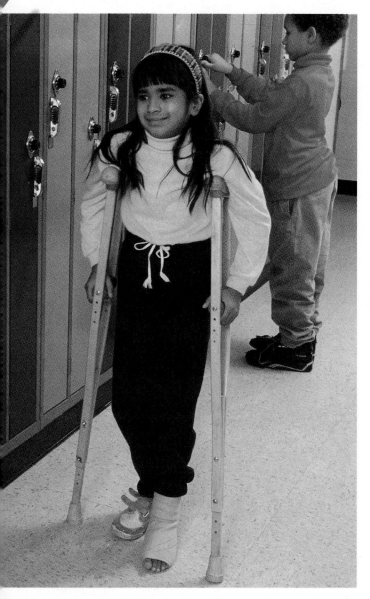

Sum It Up

Like a machine, a living thing is made of parts. If you could take an organism apart, you would find it's made of many parts. You could then take these apart and find that they are made of more parts. If you could keep taking the parts apart, you would end up with just cells. The cells go together to make parts that do the things an organism needs to live.

Critical Thinking

1. Why is it important for an organism to have parts?
2. Why don't trees need hands?
3. What parts do you have that you could live without? Why do you think that?

A toucan in Belize

Orangutans
(ô rang´ u tanz´) in
Malaysia

A rain forest in Puerto Rico

There are many different living things. But the different organisms you see today haven't always been here. At one time the only organisms on Earth had just one cell. Over many years, living things have changed to become what you see today.

The Variety Of Living Things

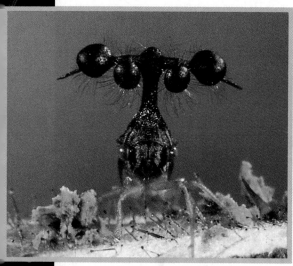

A treehopper in Brazil

How many different living things are there on Earth? You'd probably be surprised to find out there are millions! Some are bigger than a school bus. Others are tinier than a drop of water. Some are covered with fur. Others are covered with bark. All of them are different from each other in some way.

Minds On! What's the most unusual living thing you've ever seen? Maybe you saw it on television, at the zoo, or in your backyard! Draw a picture of it in your *Activity Log* on page 18 and describe it to your class. ●

Why are there so many kinds of organisms? What makes them different? These are a couple of the questions you'll be exploring in this lesson.

Activity!

Leaves Galore

You explored the parts of a plant in the last lesson. How do the parts of different plants compare? In this activity, you'll explore differences in the leaves of several plants.

What You Need

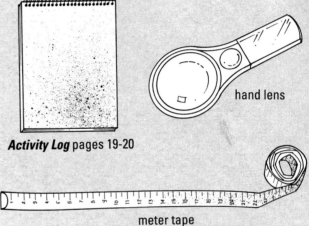

Activity Log pages 19-20

hand lens

meter tape

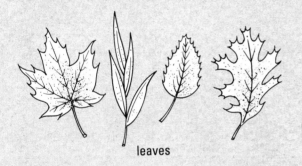

leaves

What To Do

1 Collect leaves from different trees or other plants in your neighborhood. Be careful not to remove more than one leaf from any one plant.

2 Place all the leaves on your desk.

3 Group the leaves in different ways. Try grouping them by their size, shape, color, and other ways you can think of. How are the groups different?

4 In your *Activity Log,* draw the shapes of the leaves.

5 Record the size of the leaves and any other observations.

6 Share your results with other groups.

What Happened?

1. What were the differences in size in the leaves you collected?
2. How many different shapes of leaves did you find?
3. What was the same in all the leaves you found?

What Now?

1. Why do you think the leaves are alike in some ways?
2. What differences are there among dogs? Butterflies? Birds?

EXPLORE

Differences in Living Things

All the leaves you observed were probably different in some way. They have different colors, different shapes, and different sizes. Although they all do the same things, very few plants have leaves that are the same.

Differences between things are **variations** (vâr´ ē ā´ shənz). Variations are found everywhere among living things. There are big variations, like those between plants and animals. There are also variations between similar organisms.

Lamprey

Barracuda

Gar

Catfish

Minds On! What variations are there between people? With a partner, compare your hair color, eye color, and height. Record your observations in your *Activity Log* on page 21. How do you vary from your partner? How do you vary from the rest of the class? ●

Home Is Where Your Parts Are!

The variations among organisms often allow them to live in certain places. The many different places on Earth contain many different organisms.

Some organisms can only live in certain places. If their place is changed, they may not be able to live. This is why people must try to protect all types of environments. If some environments are changed, many organisms may die. What can you do to help protect the environment?

A water dog has parts that let it get oxygen from the water it lives in.

Lizards have parts that keep them from losing water in the dry desert air.

TRY THIS Activity!

Does the Shoe Fit?

What You Need

crayons, *Activity Log* page 22

How different can feet be? The answer is only limited by your imagination. With a partner, design different feet that would be best for an organism in different places. Draw a sketch of your designs in your **Activity Log.** Write why you designed the feet that way. What are the feet good for. What are they not so good for?

Change Over Time

A trilobite (trī′ lə bĭt′) fossil

Although you designed several different feet, there are many more that walk on Earth today. Where did they all come from? Have they always been around?

There are some feet that we know don't walk on Earth anymore. These are the feet of dinosaurs. Dinosaurs haven't been around for millions of years! They are one example of how life on Earth has changed.

We know dinosaurs existed because of fossils. **Fossils** (fos′ əlz) are footprints, skeletons, or other remains of things that lived a long time ago. Much of what is known about early life on Earth has been learned by studying fossils. Scientists can find out how old a fossil is and know when that organism lived.

Minds On! Some fossils may look familiar, but others may not. Look closely at the two fossils on this page. Does either fossil look like anything you've seen before? What do you think they look like? ●

An ancient leaf fossil

Fossils show us that life has been on Earth for a long, long time. One way to understand such a long time is to use a model. Try to imagine the last 600 million years as only 12 hours. Each hour represents 50 million years. Let's look at how life has changed during the last 12 hours starting at midnight.

At 4:30 A.M.
At this time fish ruled Earth. There were many kinds, including some sharks. There were the first insects and some land plants.

At 9:00 A.M.
Large dinosaurs now rule Earth. The first palm trees and birds develop.

At 11:00 A.M.
By now there are many animals like you see today. Flowers and oak, hickory, and magnolia trees cover much of the land.

Compared to other living things, humans have walked on Earth for a very short time. Using this model, it wasn't until two and a half seconds before noon that modern humans appeared on Earth.

Although discoveries are always changing scientists' ideas, one point is clear. Life on Earth has changed greatly over time. New kinds of organisms have developed. Others have disappeared. What changes do you think the next "hour" will bring?

When Living Things Disappear

What happens to the organisms that seem to have disappeared? They have become extinct. When all of one kind of organism dies, the organism becomes **extinct** (ek stingkt´). Extinction is a natural process. It has been happening for millions of years. In fact, most living things that have been on Earth are now extinct!

Living things become extinct when their environment changes too much. The organism will die if it cannot meet its needs in the new environment. Organisms are also killed by other organisms until they become extinct.

Environments on Earth are constantly changing. Here's how one place may have changed.

Dinosaurs lived when it was warm and there was plenty of rain.

As it got colder, only organisms that could survive the ice and snow lived.

Now the environment is warmer and different organisms live on Earth.

Social Studies Link

Extinction by Humans

Humans have also played a role in the extinction of many organisms. In 1914, in a zoo in Cincinnati, Ohio, the last passenger pigeon died. The forests they lived in were cut for lumber and cleared for farms. They were also hunted for food. This has happened to many species of organisms throughout the history of humans. Can you think of some ways people can keep this from happening to other organisms?

Living Things Near Extinction

When a group of living things is in danger of becoming extinct, it is an **endangered species** (en dān´ jərd•spē´ shēz). Right now there are thousands of endangered species, and this number is getting bigger.

Minds On! What things do you know of that are endangered? Make a list in your *Activity Log* on page 23. Then, compare your list with the lists of others in your class. ●

Protected by Law

One way to prevent humans from causing the extinction of endangered species is to make laws. In 1973 the United States Congress passed the Endangered Species Act. This law makes it illegal to hunt, collect, or do anything else harmful to an endangered plant or animal.

Not everybody agrees on these laws, though. A law banning the hunting of whales caused thousands of people to lose their jobs. People have to decide which is more important—jobs or endangered species. What do you think?

The Samburu Game Preserve in Kenya

The endangered white uakari monkey in South America

Sum It Up

Earth has been the home for many different living things. During the time that life has been on Earth, it has changed a lot. Different organisms have developed over millions of years. Many kinds of living things have become extinct, too. These changes have always happened and will continue as long as Earth's environment continues to change.

Critical Thinking

1. What would Earth be like if there were no variations in living things?

2. Why can't scientists save an extinct plant or animal?

3. If you found a fossil, how would you know if that species is extinct?

The endangered white rhino in Africa

Learning from Living Things

From the peaks of its mountains to the depths of its oceans, Earth is the perfect place for life. It has water, air, and the sun nearby to provide lots of energy. There are very few places on Earth where no living things can be found. As a human, you share Earth with all other living things.

A bulldozer clearing a forest

In our efforts to meet our needs, we have placed many organisms in danger of extinction. Often this is a result of not knowing we were doing it. We have polluted the air and water, and built in areas that were once home to many living things.

We have the ability, though, to learn better ways to share Earth's resources. By learning more about the other occupants of Earth, we can do this. It is important to find out what they eat, where they live, what they do, and what they're made of.

A place to start is in your own backyard or neighborhood. Although you call it yours, many living things consider it their home, too. Find out more about whom you share your backyard with in this next activity.

TRY THIS Activity!

Backyard Wildlife

What You Need
Activity Log page 24

In your backyard, or in a nearby park, find a comfortable place to sit and observe. Watch for a while and pick one kind of organism you want to keep track of. You may choose insects, birds, or any other organism you can find. Draw it in your *Activity Log.* On seven different days, go to the same spot and observe. Don't disturb any organisms. Record how many you see, what they eat, and what they do. Using what you learned, can you think of ways you could better share the space with them?

A sand beetle in the Namib Desert in Namibia

Keeping Track Of Living Things

In doing the activity, you may have had trouble following the organisms for very long. Because they move around a lot, birds and flying insects are difficult to observe for more than a few minutes. Scientists now use all kinds of ways to follow the organisms they're studying.

One way is to attach a tiny transmitter to an animal. A **transmitter** (trans mit′ ər) is a small tag that sends out a radio signal. Using this signal, it is much easier to follow where the active animal goes and where its home is.

A transmitter has to be small and light enough for the animal to carry. It also has to be tough to "live" through everything the animal does. If the animal walks through a stream, or climbs through a pile of rocks, the transmitter needs to keep working.

The location, date of tagging, as well as other observations, are recorded. As the animal moves around, the new locations and observations are recorded. Over time a lot is learned about the movements of animals using this method.

A giraffe with a collar transmitter

Jane Goodall and Daudi Gilagaza Musa observing chimpanzees

Scientists are very interested in learning about the different organisms found on Earth. They learn about living things the same way you did—they watch them. They also study their parts to find out what they are made of. As we learn more about the other living things on this planet, we change the way we do things. These changes will hopefully avoid the unnecessary extinction of many of Earth's species.

Much has been learned about chimpanzees by watching them for many years.

GLOSSARY

Use the pronunciation key below to help you decode, or read, the pronunciations.

Pronunciation Key

a	at, bad	d	dear, soda, bad
ā	ape, pain, day, break	f	five, defend, leaf, off, cough, elephant
ä	father, car, heart	g	game, ago, fog, egg
âr	care, pair, bear, their, where	h	hat, ahead
e	end, pet, said, heaven, friend	hw	white, whether, which
ē	equal, me, feet, team, piece, key	j	joke, enjoy, gem, page, edge
i	it, big, English, hymn	k	kite, bakery, seek, tack, cat
ī	ice, fine, lie, my	l	lid, sailor, feel, ball, allow
îr	ear, deer, here, pierce	m	man, family, dream
o	odd, hot, watch	n	not, final, pan, knife
ō	old, oat, toe, low	ng	long, singer, pink
ô	coffee, all, taught, law, fought	p	pail, repair, soap, happy
ôr	order, fork, horse, story, pour	r	ride, parent, wear, more, marry
oi	oil, toy	s	sit, aside, pets, cent, pass
ou	out, now	sh	shoe, washer, fish mission, nation
u	up, mud, love, double	t	tag, pretend, fat, button, dressed
ū	use, mule, cue, feud, few	th	thin, panther, both
ü	rule, true, food	th	this, mother, smooth
ù	put, wood, should	v	very, favor, wave
ûr	burn, hurry, term, bird, word, courage	w	wet, weather, reward
ə	about, taken, pencil, lemon, circus	y	yes, onion
b	bat, above, job	z	zoo, lazy, jazz, rose, dogs, houses
ch	chin, such, match	zh	vision, treasure, seizure

allergic (ə lûr´jik) a severe response your body has to something that is harmless to other people.

allergist (al´ər jist) a doctor who helps people find what they are allergic to. They study why some people have an allergic response to something that is harmless to others.

cell (sel) basic building block of all organisms. All parts of an organism are made of cells.

conclusion (kən klü´zhən) an evaluation of whether a hypothesis is right or wrong based on experimental observations. It is the final step of scientific methods.

conserving (kən sûrv´ing) protecting Earth's resources from being lost, or ruined

consumer (kən sü´mər) an organism that cannot make its own food. Consumers get their energy by eating other organisms.

control (kən trol´) a standard of comparison used to measure or check the results

development (di vel´əp mənt) the way a living thing changes during its life

64

endangered species (en dān´jərd · spē´shēz) a group of living things in which there are very few that are living. They are in danger of becoming extinct.

experiment (ek sper´ə mənt) a test or trial to discover something. This is done to test a hypothesis when using scientific methods.

extinct (ek stingkt´) organisms that are no longer in existence. This happens when all of one kind of organism dies.

fossil (fos´əl) a footprint, skeleton, or other remains of something that was once living

grow (grō) to become larger by a natural process of development

hypothesis (hī poth´ə sis) an explanation that is based on what is already known. This is an important step in a scientific method.

mealworm (mēl´wûrm) a small worm-like organism, or larva, that later develops into a Tenebrio beetle

organism (ôr´gə niz´əm) a living thing

oxygen (ok´sə jən) a colorless, odorless, tasteless gas found in air and water. It is needed by all living things.

problem (prob´ləm) a question that needs to be solved. This is the first step in using scientific methods.

producer (prə dü´sər) an organism that makes its own food. Plants are producers that make food using sunlight, carbon dioxide and other nutrients.

record (ri kôrd´) to write observations down so they can be used later

reproduce (rē´prə düs´) to make new living things of the same kind

resource (rē´sôrs´) materials from Earth that people use

response (ri spons´) something a living thing does when its environment changes. Shivering when you're cold is a response.

scientific method (sī ən tif´ik · məth´əd) a way scientists solve problems. It usually has five steps—stating the problem, forming a hypothesis, experimenting, recording observations, making a conclusion

transmitter (tranz mit´ər) a small tag attached to an animal that sends out a radio signal to keep track of the animal

variation (vâr´ē ā´shən) a difference between two or more things

INDEX

CREDITS